Dust and Bread

Also by Stephen Haven:

Poetry
The Long Silence of the Mohawk Carpet Smokestacks (2004)

Memoir
The River Lock: One Boy's Life Along the Mohawk (2008)

Translations
The Enemy in Defensive Positions: Poems from China (Editor
        and co-translator, 2008)

Anthologies
And What Rough Beast: Poems at the End of the Century (Co-
        editor, 1999)
Scarecrow Poetry: The Muse in Post-Middle Age (Co-editor,
        1994)
The Poetry of W.D. Snodgrass: Everything Human (Editor,
        1993)

Dust and Bread

Poems by Stephen Haven

Turning Point

Published by Turning Point
P.O. Box 541106
Cincinnati, OH 45254-1106

ISBN: 1932339027
LCCN: 2008900011

Poetry Editor: Kevin Walzer
Business Editor: Lori Jareo

Visit us on the web at www.turningpointbooks.com

Cover art: *Toward the Blue Peninsula*, 1951-52 by Joseph Cornell, Construction, 10 5/8 x 14 5/16 x 3 15/16 inches, Collection Daniel Varenne, Geneva © The Joseph and Robert Cornell Memorial Foundation/Licensed by VAGA, New York, NY

Acknowledgment is made to the following journals for poems that appeared previously in their pages:

American Poetry Review: "A Geography of Movement"
Artful Dodge: "Willow"
The Cincinnati Review: "The Word *Wonders*"
The Clackamas Literary Review: "Blossom," "Sun Wukong, Monkey King," "Ultrasound"
The Dickinson Review: "Summer in a Large House"
Ekphrasis: "New World," "*Toward the Blue Peninsula*"
The Fourth River: Nature and Culture: "If China Is a Willow," "Skunked"
Hellas: "The Sympathy of Trees" appeared in earlier form under the title "The Trees Are Simply Ordinary"
Image: A Journal of the Arts and Religion: "Another Genesis," "Homage to Gregory Gillespie," "Toward a Definition of Home"
The Journal: "Waxing," "*Slow It Down, Baby!*"
Literary Imagination: "Cat's Paw"
PIF Magazine: "Miao Village, Hainan Island," "Gold Mountain," and "Headache, PRC"
Poetry Miscellany: "Mao's Sparrows," "Temple of Heaven"
Salmagundi: "Homage to Agee," "W.D. Snodgrass and the Owl"
Southern Indiana Review: "Hornets' Nest"
The Texas Review: "Cello," "Hawthorn," "Cutting the Tree"
Western Humanities Review: "Zoo"

"Blue Flame" appeared solo during Christmas week 2006 on the literary web-zine *whyareweiniraq.com*

"Ultrasound" was reprinted in the anthology *Family Matters: Poems of Our Families,* edited by Ann Smith and Larry Smith (Bottom Dog Press, 2005).

"Blossom" and "Sun Wukong, Monkey King" were reprinted in *Imported Breads: Literature of Cultural Exchange,* ed. Philip Sterling (Mammoth Books, 2003).

"Waxing" was reprinted in Chinese translation in *World Literature* (Beijing, 2000).

Portions of "Hornets' Nest" appear in Catherine Kirby's digital collage, "Hornets' Nest."

"Elegy for Larry Levis" appears in the anthology *And What Rough Beast: Poems at the End of the Century* (Ashland Poetry Press, 1999).

Thanks to the Ohio Arts Council, the Fulbright Foundation, the MacDowell Arts Colony, the Yaddo Foundation, and the Provincetown Fine Arts Work Center for grants and residencies that supported the writing of many of these poems.

For Sarah and Jonah

***

An Awe if it should be like that
Upon the Ignorance steals—

—Dickinson, Poem 575

Contents

I. Beijing

Willow

All China a green-gold row of them.
When you walk through—
delicate, skirted, light-limbed

and yellow, swishing their loveliness
in the wind—they brush
the whole of you.

The Han are awfully dark
to love such hair: one single tree
the parasol of thousands

of years of poetry.
It is essentially
a pastoral tradition, a light

gesture in a concrete sea—
this park, these willows,
these bamboo growing near,

as if forever curtained
beneath these trees
Li Bai still sprung

pure passion from a flush of wine.
And if you listen
you can almost hear him:

bamboo, bamboo, the green shoots
of earth, heaven when they brush
these yellow skirts!

Sun Wukong, Monkey King

I come to see him often, bike it past
Tiananmen and Mao's mausoleum,
and the monochromatic, rectangular

downtown grey Soviet architecture
to where the pagodas
of the pre-Communist theater district

curl skyward the fandangos
of their brilliant eaves. Tonight,
it's Sun Wukong, the Monkey King,

on stage. I first heard of him
in the nervous recitation
of a five-year-old girl

(my wife did the translation).
I know how he was hatched
from a stone womb, a monkey statue

until the mechanical
movement of the season
slipped five fen in the slot machine

of destiny and heaven (the stars
aligned, his cold eyes glowed,
two red coals). Beloved

of China, star
of the Beijing Opera,
he's the self-proclaimed "Great Sage,

Equal to Heaven," a cloud leaper
evolved out of nothing
and master of 72 transformations.

***

It isn't especially a religious country.
Still, in every season,
the people flock to see him:

"Wukong and the Arhats,"
"Wukong and the Demon King."
Little flames of black flicker up

from lips to cheeks to pointed ears.
Fidelity and treachery—red and white—
streak the permanent laughter of his face.

Then the erhu whines, the xiaoluo, those high
pitched cymbals, punctuate each wide-eyed
mischievous turning of his mind.

Wukong begins his eternal shenanigans,
crashing, jealous uninvited guest,
the annual heavenly peaches festival:

Plucking three hairs from his head,
he blows on them and three
mosquitoes bite each of the immortals.

They're sleeping deeply by the time
he staggers on the stolen wine.
Then, as he somersaults out of heaven,

just before he offers, for longevity's sake,
sacks of that immortal fruit
to his loyal legions of earthly primates,

15

two phoenixes, his cousins in vertigo,
rise above two dragons, their feathered
rainbows shimmering, their tails on fire.

***

It does no good to say, I would eat too
if Wukong, troubled mortal,
sick with the seed of heaven in him,

came down off of center stage
and reached into the foreigner's section,
the best seats in the house,

and laughed and pawned that fruit of life
at a higher than reasonable price.
In the battle to defeat him,

the victorious Wukong
(a momentary victory), twirls
his cudgel as a majorette her baton.

There is no need to show—everyone knows—
how he loses in the end,
how in the one crucial moment,

grieving for the masses
of mortal monkeys bleeding or dead,
doubt reconnoiters him. Powerless

to kill him, heaven burns and buries him
for a thousand years beneath
the Buddha's hand, Five Fingers Mountain.

***

Then past the touristic, miniature opera masks
and silk embroidered cushion covers,
past the overpriced, ink still lifes

to where my bicycle—a *Phoenix*,
not a *Flying Pigeon* or a *Butterfly*—
is locked outside. It is February,

it is five in the evening.
There are hundreds of thousands,
even millions of *Phoenixes*.

We glide, almost invariably black,
along the hutongs, our wings
spread in one mass, past the mounds

of coal dust, which lie untouched till spring
but still swirl up like snow
or some blown dandelion gone to seed

when the wind comes down off the Gobi.
I think of you, Wukong, Great Sage,
of that mountain off your back,

and everywhere in Beijing, across
the city, one thousand years
drift, lifeless and grey as this spent ash.

—In memory of the Tiananmen massacre

Ultrasound

To my daughter, five months before her birth
in Beijing, Spring Festival, 1991

The Chinese half of your family counts
the curled time inside the womb.
You're four months old.

Your mother sings, not exactly to you,
on Lunar New Year's Eve,
on the piano,

a song her father wrote
years ago (it once pleased Mao):
 Little Buddhas of peeled apples

and oranges in a bowl
and a nasal, pentatonic vibrato
echoing off the concrete walls.

But there's another echo too,
some silence stuffed
down your mother's throat

as she sings this song her father wrote.
All the other women, seventy years
between them, stop for a moment

pinching dumplings into crescents.
Only one young uncle falls asleep,
his face gone purple with grief and baijiu,

his one son lost shoveling coal
at the Beijing Duck Hotel,
then biking home, after dark, past

Tiananmen, June 4th.
Anniversary of absences,
song of a night to be sad.

Someone recalls, now, on his birthday,
in prison, your mother's father was given
one boiled goose egg.

The dry black husks of watermelon seeds
scatter the slab floor. And all the while,
outside the living room's one window

the moon refuses to show,
masked in clouds and the earth's shadow,
its power magnified behind a shroud.

Begonias of violence, man-powered stars
burst their last cartwheels
in a long rumor of dawn.

All night tonight, even in translation,
the musicians who betrayed him,
grieve or say nothing:

In the loneliness
of their lit stage, in the posthumous concert
where they rehabilitated his name,

the music ricocheted
stray bullet
shot in the dark.

***

What is the pact we make with you?
We wait for you.
Yesterday, at the Beijing Capital Hospital,

we looked in to see, five months early,
you, floating in your beginning.
The peninsular pieces of yourself

were grotesque in their separate whorls.
Your heart splashed in front of us
like mercury on glass,

your spine was a toothed grin.
And where there might have been a grin—
a mouth, something—

the faceless contours of your head
stared back as blank and knowing
as some extraterrestrial's

wondrous descent to where we live.
Quartered in the lilliputian monitor,
archipelago in the rising

of everything we couldn't see,
the pure promise of a seed
and the nightmare of leprosy

were unfolding there
as they will here
but gently now, I promise you,

in unison, in the open air.

If China Is a Willow

all Britain is an oak.
Of course the season falls,
the last leaf kicks
back to mother dirt. So long,
that year, Hong Kong. Small con-
solation, the law that says
even hardwood rots
and who knows what
the brown-capped seeds
might touch? Now we hear
the language inscribed
on the ancient coin of power
everywhere. The stubborn
stump springs one new leaf.

What else is printed there?
What else when in the rain
the sawdust becomes
the pulp of some new page?
It tears, and the birds
of words that once built
their nests there
lift like ripped stitches
against the autumn sky,
the rush of their light
bones more lovely
than the undulations
of a songbird's throat.

Almost palpably
in proportion to the power
of the performer, the moment
just after. That year
only a young poet heard

who sat beneath a willow
each day it rained.
He ate his lunch of cold pork
from a tin box. We gaped
at each other like simpletons.
Still, he knew the word
for friend in two languages
and took me once to see
the old calligrapher
who with sponge and stick
and water, wrote
each Sunday on the walks
of Bahai Park. As we watched,

a crowd gathered around
until there was nothing there
but the brush of what someone
hushed into grace, once,
a violence that had lifted
momentary on the air.

Another Genesis
for Jing Jing, and for our boy

Before the drip of pitocin
stopped our talk, you joked of Eve,
the apple, of that one bite
and you were stuck with an epidural.

We thought she might have done
better to consult a lawyer,
to negotiate, at the very least,
an exemption for women
of different origins,
for you, for all Chinese.

God was plainly not PC.

I quoted Isaiah, chapter 44,
verse 2, "I am He that formed
thee in thy mother's womb."

Pressed to make conversation
I improvised another version,
some gnostic silence
penetrating heaven
and we had Eden, its placenta

a river pulsing
from the still center,
to feed, as rivers do,
to water, to make things grow.

Then Exodus: the blood
of the final push,
the Red Sea parting, issuing
out and out...

You were lost by then.
We spoke of simple things,
of breath and its consequences.

Then sleep. Then the final letting go,
the rhythm of pain coming harder,
opening to exhaustion, to the price
of love—blood—and something slower

a momentary loss—
a lifetime or so—
of some old self-conception
of ourselves. When our boy,

when our soaked Jonah eased out
like a piece of rolled meat,
a regular tenderloin,
shoulders curled so that they
almost touched, chin tucked,

we knew right then just what we were,
knew it was religion,
its work, its aspiration,
the body broken, breaking,
the blood poured out
                        eternity itself—
or something like it—
glinting in and out of view
in the double black-brown crystal,
the deep translucence
of a one-day old.

Temple of Heaven

There, in the Hall of Prayer, under the Good
Harvest Dome, even the emperors
planted in whispers seeds that might rise

through concentric circles to the sky.
They were the prayers they breathed,
the central pillars of the point toward which

our tour guide let us lean, not sit.
The entire temple was a times table,
nine fan-shaped slabs

in the top-most inner ring,
the second with two times nine,
third three times. Until at the center

of the bottom-most eighty-one
everything depended, the testosterone
of the throne, the hunger of the people,

on that flaccid number's masculine design.
The throne was roped off, but in that 9 x 9,
we could see the exact point where earth

touched sky: vats of gathered rice and wheat,
gored pigs and sheep on the engraving
of the clipped wings of September,

corn-fattened flocks on the ninth
of the twelve pillars. Within eternity's
nine circles, we imagined them imagining.

Then 1999 lifted its angles against the sky
like monuments some Muscovite mob
never traveled East to tear down:

A small crowd gathered around two ehrus,
old men who whined with bow and string
and not for money, for no one's pleasure,

as far as I could see, but their own
beneath the trees. Through the haze
of that grey evening, my wife and I saluted

and clowned with Mao caps on,
posed for money in the Empress's
and Emperor's gowns,

snapped and flashed away at the new tiger
of the Chinese yuan. Then, tired at last,
we tipped our glasses and filled them again

as the night snapped on: downtown's
monolithic slabs, pure concrete,
capped like bad teeth

with pagodas or the ghostly shape of them,
their wings made wholly of wire and light.
We talked of Mao, of beauty, its price,

its presence too in this dark matter
of food, and wondered what he'd say,
preserved in the polished monotony

of his own infallible decay.
(He whispered from his glass coffin
of the kiss that might wake him.)

Gate of Good Harvest, Hall of Abstinence,
in such a house, who would throw
a stone? You nod toward the yellow

arches of McDonald's now! But even
the architecture, swollen in time's
mundane swagger, wouldn't wish them

back again, these emperors
who killed millions, who kept as slaves
thousands of women, eunuchs to herd them,

and had prepared 99 dishes
for each Royal New Year!
Over noodles and dumplings,

history's downward imperious curve
beaded in the sweat of our *Yanjing* beer.
We wondered what it said for them

that at the center of such grace,
only in the wash of beauty,
they prayed for their people's rice.

Hornets' Nest

It's as if a filament of hornets
somehow mirrored us
and we gape, as we do mornings,

at the buzzing bulbs
of our own heads,
some inner owl of us calling.

But now, in the rain, the papery grey
Chinese lantern of a nest
hangs some twenty feet above us:

A bonnet of stings, out
on a limb, so that we can imagine
desire beyond the near border

of fear, some pure potential
for violence that has brought us
to stand here. Twenty years ago

I would have Big Banged
that black hole. Older now,
I leave well enough alone.

But once they claimed the eaves
of my childhood home:
Young and limber, I climbed

the three stories for my father
and shot (in their still night)
the poison in. We are their match

in ferocity. Ants in our beams,
rugs full of fleas, ground water
in the cellar, all nature conspires

to elbow in
to our square footage.
We conspire to edge in the dream

of domesticity, a Chinese lantern
trimmed just right or its glow
might bring down a house!

Our neighbors whisper at the buzz
of our own home. We go out
in the rain, and building, building

find there the compressed
restless energy
that makes a nest.

Blossom

April, late afternoon,
the long lawn of the Summer Palace
a thatched basket of shadows…

We sit awhile above
the late light bouncing off the water,
cascading up the bridge's tiled arc.

I don't know which empress built
this manmade channel,
don't care to reconstruct

the naked eunuchs lounging here
or down below
where the water pools

into each separate dynasty,
Sung and Ming and Qing—
I can't keep track of them—

and each boat's launched
with the same bow,
an imperial, jade dragon's fiery mouth.

What can a tourist know? The past
is made of stone. Silently,
in its native tongue, the immutable

moment hushes its orphaned sons.
On our way out we stop to listen,
stop to watch statuesque women

posing for their men,
their sleek black hair brushed back,
softened with the spilled

light of the season,
their hands outstretched to blossoms—
dwarf peach, magnolia—

as if their husbands' instamatics
had caught their assured, far off gazes
only by chance,

and it all belonged naturally to them,
the grounds no longer forbidden,
as if to say, *me too, if the magnolias can!*

Gold Mountain

There on the Hudson, the lower west side
of Manhattan, we sailed a slow sail,
the sun half an hour high,
the water glassy, then dead, and then
though we hadn't once thought of her
suddenly she appeared
floating filthy on the water,
the lit woman, an immigrant herself,
fire of the crowd who built
effigies in her name, paraded her
at Tiananmen, and when the dying came
burned with her like papier-mâché.
I had never yearned to see that fire,
never ferried out in a crowded boat
to touch the skirt of desire itself,
but then I found myself that evening,
for pleasure only, on a small sailboat:

Except for me we were all Chinese:
Gold Mountain they still call it
though what has it meant more
than a wilderness named New York,
the sight of such a mythic beauty
rising suddenly into view,
the harbor arcing toward Ellis,
the sun half an hour high?
Then ferried over the darkened water
only to find that heaven, suddenly,
pulled up stakes and moved
on down the road,
always to the next and next
western town. Until they let it go,
came to call one world home.
So close, so far, they could still,

in their dreams, smell the sea,
but landlocked in memory
burning with the fire
of a hand rising out of winter water.

Gold Mountain. Boston. Quetzalcoatl.
Miami Beach. Venus will never rise
on a half shell in New York Harbor.
But when Liberty herself slips into view
and a woman, light years away
from her father's grave,
leans the luxuriance of her dark hair
over your left shoulder
and crosses with you
the chained bay waters, the spun
space between two worlds, the distance
of continents buoying you up?
You take her home, a place
you once knew, and shed
your clothes, and in the ten-year drift
of an evening, grow toward the sheer promise

of silk alley, the merchants stamping
their feet to keep off the cold,
the hawked lust of a good deal,
silk and leather and down,
clouding the air.
The woman, your wife by then,
once waited there.
Outside the American Embassy
on a pre-dawn January morning
she brought you once to see:

Tail in its mouth,
the line snaked all the way around
the block. Then the light broke
on Beijing, then they were already
whispering her name: *Gold Mountain*

we almost heard them say
though she is made of stone.
Who would be so quick
to doubt the worth of it?
Drifting, drifting, already gone,
they waited there, as if they had
a prayer, as if the idea of it
were lasting and true
though they were ever casting off
further and further from the known world.

II. Let Us Now Praise Famous Men

Homage to Agee

What right did that man have to put my picture
on the cover of his book?
                —Clare Belle Ricketts

Somehow you slipped into their lives,
your car, your parachute of dust
a long way off and then the barefoot
children running up, their fathers
close behind, nodding their heads,
grinning and all the while
watching you with the backs of their eyes.
A few small peaches were warming in a tin
in the sun of that first meeting,
the threads of heat like rising smoke,
the land all distance, cotton undergrowth,
and faraway pine, faraway sky. Just why
those Alabamians took you in,
in greed or kindness offered you
their bare wood kitchens, bug-infested beds,
eggs fried in year-old fat,
grits and greens and chicken backs,
I don't suppose you yourself would know.
Somehow they simply trusted you
on that first day when you guffawed
and grinned, became a down-home
boy again, and through the smoke screen
of your talk, lined them up, half-believing,
before the hole of Evans' camera. I don't doubt

you tried to stare beyond yourself,
to see them as they really were
and not as you imagined them.
But other things kept creeping in,
that star-like bruise gathered at the tip
of your father's chin:

Dead when you were six years old,
he followed you, glided with your shadow,
even there in Shady Grove.
When you thought of him,
it was the pure soprano of a boy
breaking in the body of a man.

And the quiet of what that thin voice meant—
detrital, resonant—did it lull you as you stayed
up late, read and wrote, and by the front
porch lamp, by the open door,
rocked in the underworld a small flame threw?
The slightest of those farmers' things,
a mason jar of sorghum, one child's
brown cotton glove,
whispered their hollowed human names.
It must have been plain
to some of them, you knew something
of what love is: distant, a hymn we hear
yet can't quite sing,
the cabin gone to silence, to night
and Alabama and all the world asleep.

Snowed-in with the Bishop,
Confirmation Day

Then, suddenly, for three blown days, he slept in
          our home.
It snowed and snowed. At first, he tried to slip away,
swerved once or twice like a regular guy, then slowed
on the New York Thruway. Until the weather held him,
as earlier he had held us, with a silence, a presence.
In the vestibule, the Bishop abandoned his
          pontificals.

Perhaps there was a silence in the Bishop's pontificals
as they hung in the front door hallway of our home.
Perhaps a quiet gathered there, perhaps one sense
of memory, spun in the closeted dark, one formal way
of living, made of that mauve thread, one hymn
too difficult to sing, one rainbow of everything he sowed.

But in the living room, sheltered from the snow,
I didn't think of the Bishop's bright pontificals.
Or how, as if he fixed a stamp there, his washed thumb
had creased the foreheads of the kneeling young. *Home,
          home,*
that liturgical man droned, home was cocooned in us,
          always.
In the living room, I was confirmed again with presents.

Everything outdoors halted before that blinding presence.
Now, the snow said numbly, fallen and falling, *now, now.*
There was nothing to do but shovel and cut wood,
          the driveway
buried in drifts. Fire and snow were the winter's
          pontificals.

When we were stripped of our wet clothes, we were
          finally home.
Mom cracked the rum: O.K.! the Bishop signaled with
          his thumb.

The hours turned back on themselves. The snowplows
          hummed,
the chains around their tires ringing with a common sense.
But those drawn days, something uncommon was in
          our home
where we dealt the Queen of Spades, dark cousin of
          the snow,
the Bishop in my father's robe, his new maroon
          pontificals.
We hoped it would snow and snow, that he wouldn't
          go away.

The Hearts, the board games, the fire said *This is the Way.*
And what the rising and falling wind whipped up
          was a hymn
caught in glass, barring and calling us, ponderous, fickle.
Only the distant plows churned to the sound of dollars,
          cents.
The Bishop never spoke of Cain and Abel, Jacob
          and Esau,
of them in him and he in us inside our snowed-in home.

We each gave him a present before he went away.
Drive slow! we hymned, gleaming from the porch of our
          warm home.
The only color in the snow, the shock of his pontificals.

Homage to Gregory Gillespie

The point of abstraction, the way you hedged
your bets, was the perfect portrait
of a watermelon, curved and veined until
it gelled into a human brain.
Or it was Rita, your wife's grandmother,
mad by the time you painted her,
a waft of hair luxuriating
from her chin. On the verge
of her own becoming, you gave yourself
fully to the blind eye of the mole
that lightly stares beneath
one gaping nostril. If that was love,
it was nothing personal,
the magma of each slow wrinkle
in the last eruption of a life.

Or else yours was a wilder gambit, a gambler's
sleight of hand, to site the gem
of each object's cut edge
along its million dollar mark.
In the sapphire of each familiar thing,
the semblance of the spirit, the rind of it,
were lambent with one another,
like an otter in water.
Under a magnifying mirror,
in some slight aberration of eye or glass,
you tracked a theology of skin,
each pore, each follicle, guiding you
as if, with a triple-zero brush,
you might, like some Thomas, stick
an appendage in. The point of abstraction,

the way you struck your line, was where
the veneer of the physical spun like a fly
fisherman's reel. Nose to nose with the dog-
breath of each detail, each object
a gift horse looked hard in the mouth,
until, by the neck, in your own studio,
you became a thing yourself. The question
was never whether that horse would win,
but when, on the last furlong,
it would fall, while the jockey saw
not the crowd, not the cool millions
gone to hay, but the close up rain
of earth, each particle of this fast world
in some strange oasis gone suddenly slack…
Each self-portrait stares back.

Skunked

They mug right in like innocence itself,
these nocturnal Napoleons:
Some sweetness made wholly
of August and air, and the crust
of Ohio, lures them into the glow
of your kitchen window.

But how strange to carry, on your body,
a small piece of the highway,
white-split blacktop
signaling the world to pass.
Stick your nose right in and the traffic
of all humanity veers like the Red Sea,
and face it, baby, you ain't no Moses…

From the lit interior of your dirty dishes,
you can hear them clicking
against the canned swill of your day.
But then the curve of ignominy rears
as you tap the glass. For the first time,
you realize, there is, on the backside,

no single stripe, only an elliptical white,
black hole of the middle, shape of our own
orbit. It narrows to a close
at the humped shoulders, squat of the tail.

By now, you are sure where they will birth
the next generation. You do not want
to fight them beneath the floorboards
of your porches: fire with fire, castor oil,
moth balls by the dozens to burn
the delicate fibers inside their sinuses…

You remember, now, that in the reformation
of each worn morning, Martin Luther
stared at the rosary of the curds
issuing from his own body. What other
nourishment had soured there?

For this the universe has the skunk.
From either side of the rectum,
it shoots its musk fifteen feet out.

Secretly, now, you will stock the larder
with peroxide, rosemary, white vinegar.
When the lights go down, when love
tucks itself safely in, the skunk forages…

Dump the tar, dump the feathers…
This is what shame must be:
the smeared stench of the berm
pulsing near your home,
a claw's faint tattoo…

W.D. Snodgrass and the Owl

In every way but genetically he fathered a bird.
He showed me photographs of the owlet,
half-grown, wing-tucked, perched on
his leather-clad arm, then of the grown
in full flight, five-foot wings
flapping like two flags from a distant country,
claws outstretched as it struck and struck.

When the bird could finally kill, when some slight
fear of humankind glinted in its stone eye,
he let it go. The owl returned
one year in spring, nested in his backyard
hemlock tree. It called down less mechanically
than the other birds, *who, who, who,*
its voice almost heavenly.

Because I knew there can be, of course,
no answer, when from the sky in spring
a familiar, almost heavenly voice
descends on wings,
I never asked him how he knew
it was, that year, truly the one same bird
he'd raised up from the human world.

Evening on evening, that sung season,
unpruned under the unpruned apple trees,
the poet sprawled out, a lanky six-foot even,
and deeply listened: His desire took wing,
soared above the cropless farms
yawning all around, above the horses, cows,
the two silos gracing the distance, night coming on,

and then returned to that same lofty perch
where, below, the one earth-bound father
listened with a little awe
and not without a touch of fear,
while the bird, the thing he had made,
called down again, *who, who, who,*
always that same unanswerable question.

Elegy for Larry Levis

One last cigarette, then,
in the rigor mortis of his lips
and all he has to say is this:

drift, drift.

He was almost young.
One didn't have to know him well
one didn't have to love his poetry to feel
the indigenous weight of it.

A drop of Spanish blood.

Now, if he sings of California,
Lorca's black elf
grins over his left shoulder.

De Soto, floating in his ossuary,
whistles through cracked teeth.

Tonight his work in the form
of a moth on a dark sill,
moth on the mouth of where
he'd ever been. Or else the poem

of his old age,
a mythic vintage,
year that will never come.

The quiet of his voice, tonight:

Cognac, cognac on the tongue.

Toward the Blue Peninsula
after Joseph Cornell

You can't ignore the curved, single white
feather blending to the blank, white wall
or the one, brown, wooden corner bench
for waiting on. Bars, bars everywhere—
One overhead, one along the floor
are acts of kindness on the keeper's part:
The men who stayed here, did they grunt and work
their abdomens and arms? Then catch the view
stunning from the peeled-back grate of the window?
Even inaudibly, *beyond, beyond, beyond,*
sings the guttural, billion-year-old sea.

Eternity is boring, but who can keep
from counting it on his sore fingertips?
A broken dish, a milk-white, chipped
water glass. It's easiest to say
these are the nondescript accouterments
of someone else's cell—say, Icarus,
who with his father cut the window's wire
and, rushed, caught a wing-tip as he leapt
into the blue of the all outdoors, sky
and waves, though here and there a wisp of clouds,
white caps and mist along the swallowing sea.

Or else, beyond the water, because the view
leans toward the unseen peninsula,
Ponce de Leon: *his* dream, *his* day in the sun.
Too frightening to think it is your own
Florida seen here, where, grown old,
you aim your striped umbrella at the sun.
Almost angry, impatient for the thrill
the gleaming, bleached bone of the white hotel

promised you, you're unseen on the patio.
The hard, black disc of shuffleboard spins then rests.
The one reprieve from the murmur of the blue, blue sea.

New World

Joseph Cornell's *Bébé Marie*

A hat of straw's strapped on her head, its ribbon
mixed with leaves, her inconspicuous hair
sifts down the barren twigs like winter foliage.
Hidden back behind the tangled branches,
she just stares. She never says a word.

And all around the dominating shades
of threatening skies: black and grey and yet
my eye is drawn to a line of light that frames
the redness of her cheeks, her yellow hat.
Looking closer, now, I see her eyes

are deep, deep brown or the same black. She stares.
The forest grows. She stares. Beyond the twigs
that brush her hair, beyond her speckled box,
an omnipresent wood lies like a stark
and open sea where all horizons are false.

A Geography of Movement

They migrated to fill their needs, the south Texas
         aborigines.
Each move was woven to the thin web
of food and fuel, shelter and clothing
and desire circling among them like a renegade slave.

Now their eventual movement to nothingness
is a fossil in a Spaniard's book:
Cabeza de Vaca wrote everything we know of them
seven years after his raft broke up at Galveston.

It was inland for prickly pears and then
wintering for clams.
It was taking shelter in their grass huts
when the sky pulsed purple and the tornado struck.

Then, when they demanded it of his white skin,
he found that he could heal them,
found he was a Christian, and grew to love
them and God and the laying on of hands.

A kind of Messiah to them, naked, bearded,
he led masses of those first Americans
down to Mexico, 1537,
where fearing their loyalty only to him, the lesser

authorities had them slaughtered or enslaved.

***

Movement has its infinite directions,
De Vaca sent back to Spain in chains.
Who knows if it were determined that way

51

or if this and everything happens by accident
so that even the miracles he turned for them—

cutting an arrow tip out from a man—
had nothing of the Grace of God,
no cross connection between dimensions,
and except for the one human outstretched hand,
nothing of Michelangelo's "Adam."

Nothing, in other words, of the bread of heaven,
that one sure fuel of mass movement,
though people will discover it where they will:
two thousand years of melting on the tongue
the tasteless round white wafer of God.

Or further back than that, in some prehistoric
accident, when oiled in the open bowl,
the unleavened flour, wet and heavy,
waiting to be born again
in fire for the first time rose:

And around the mouth of the oven
the stunned people gathering like children
at the first sight of snow—
Did they think it might restore
the godhead in them? And what if it did?

***

Even in that first earthly notion of heaven,
before the apple, before the serpent,
the place laden with fruit and water,
straw for their bed, a canopied weave
of branches for a roof where they slept,

still the first man and the first woman
walked to work the fields each morning,
though the garden was perfect
and there was nothing they could do
to improve or harm it,

a maze of swallows knifing overhead,
the doe-eyed lion pacing with the lamb.
They knew, and more so later,
the world was in motion and so moved with it.
Moving, they were more at home in it.

III. Grace Notes

Love's a Cut Engine, Anchored
or Drifting

I have listened, in the water, on my back,
ears under, when the Sacandaga Reservoir's
a conch whose shell is mountains,
whose sound's the drummer's
lightest touch, a cymbal barely brushed.

So I float a little into myself
and it's nowhere near enough.

And always this amniotic prayer,
always beneath me
down at the other end
of the chained buoy,
the weight that keeps our boat circling.

Always the desire
to stay awhile longer.

So I do, an extra few minutes or so:
Above all else, I love the windpipe
of myself, and outboards
buzzing no louder than a bee
drugged by the way
the planet tilts
each fall night toward ice.

Waxing

We just have to crawl our way through
like earth worms drilling apples
only higher and perfectly peeled.
There are stars within such cores
and the seeds are for swallowing.
Tunnel through or swallow the moon!
When you can't see beyond the visible,
when no one leaf formally finishes itself
up among the scattered stars,
go out, at night, and walk.
The moon exists from all sides at once:
Blind eye, sinkhole, searchlight.

The Sympathy of Trees

We are right to build our homes with them,
to listen when the weather's catching
in the eaves, whole buildings
shifting a little in their frames,
bending and pulling back again
the way, in storms, the sea will lift
a ship one moment out of its own element...

Tonight, I'm sitting beneath the trees
and though they're caught in the ground
waist-deep, though the birds,
the lightest of their leaves,
come close but can't quite teach
the rigidity of limbs
the sudden up-sweep of their wings,

I'm wondering how I ever questioned
the muted gift hidden within us,
when here, in my own backyard,
through the lesser instruments
of wood and sap and green,
the wind is seen, the invisible
orchestrates its name.

Headache, PRC

My first week in Beijing, no fever,
my sinuses pounding: The campus doctor
figures my addiction's aspirin.
OK, I take a lot of them.
I ask for two. Suddenly
it's group therapy, it's Bastille Day
at the People's University.
Students from the hallway
elbow in. True to our bred natures,
each of us curious,
I'm the bearded lady, the big nose;
they are the green chorus,
the canned laughter at this show.
Then my wife concurs.
It is a serious disease.
Whatever song they're singing
it's in unison and sways
her. She speaks for me.
Eight years away she's come home
a Beijing girl, a woman of her word.
If only it were singular!
I have had enough when she agrees
there must be blood—mine—
two vials to measure
the effects of such a potent drug.
No problem, the doctor tells me,
he'll take care of everything:
the needle's sterile, if not
disposable. *No worry, No worry.*
I turn to walk away: *OK,* he says
OK, and gives me two, and a cup
of boiled water, all to the silent
leer of the crowd. Then says
he wouldn't touch me now,

I couldn't pay. He'd have to throw
away the needle. He's afraid of AIDS,
the wild veins that have branched across
the sea, and for all he knows
sit before him now.
Two aspirin won't do it now,
the water so hot I must sip.
I swallow. My wife glares.
The tablets aren't coated and stick.

Miao Village, Hainan Island

The women like nuns or 17th century Puritans
except for the embroidered flash
of bonnets that drew us on.

They waved green shoots of bamboo:
no photographs unless we paid.
Little girls dressed the same,

black blouses, skirts, mini almost.
Pigs locked in bamboo pens,
their piglets running free,

and turkeys gripped, it seemed,
by some deep inner shiver
(it was centigrade 40 degrees),

tensing their feathers,
their warty bills,
their whole bodies in warning.

When we had our fill, when we turned
to go, I pressed 5 quai into the hand
of the loveliest, the oldest,

a woman so bent she trailed the rest,
and scattered 10 fen bills,
2 cents American, to the youngest girls.

And suddenly they were on me,
flash of color, flash and flash,
like some starved goldfish

out of a black mass.
I tossed another handful,
this time to the wind, and sent them,

for a moment only, flurrying after them.
Then word spread: dozens more
out of doors, drumming at my legs,

fingering me, a problem
beyond money. Then one woman slipped—
I remember it was the left—breast

back in, her baby in one arm,
and slapped me hard on the ass.
But my wife would not be driven back

to our bus like an animal to the barn.
There was some snarl left in the Chinese,
tourists too, come down from Beijing:

They were half annoyed, half amused to see
the bus driver knocking down some baijiu
with his beer, though it was a narrow road

through the mountains back to Haiko.
Or these children, in their native dress,
picking an old wound, the Christians

driven off the land 50 years ago.
One last splash of cash
and I saw them as they took flight,

anywhere that faith and funds
would carry them, how they blessed
the crops, and peeled the youngest

children off, like some old scab, so clean,
so easy. New wounds bleed, their pilot
banking the plane into the wind,

our bus driver honking like mad,
slipping some near collision
into the opposite lane.

We leaned into each other
each of us rocked in our seats,
giddy with laughter by then,

what we were, thought we were,
giving ourselves to the rush
of the oncoming trucks.

Cello

I really only learned to play
a movement or two of some
suite for unaccompanied cello.

Mainly etudes in solitude.

Still, my fingers bled for you.
Even off key, my body swayed
from C to A when I bit in

at the base of the bow
and sent in a double stop
the power of some simple Bach

quivering to the top of your scroll!
My cello, between us
it was something physical:

You were a pulsing thing,
a melancholy levity—
drawn hair, thick *largo*—

I hugged between my legs.
My scratchy love,
my public albatross,

I played you only in private
like a fat spouse.
Then, in sixteen years, I never

touched you once, lugged you,
a promise I made to myself
from house to house to house.

When I let you go
sold you last December
for some unpaid bill or the other

your absence in my home
was a closet that filled quickly
like a dent in dough.

Now I wish for you what I might wish
for any quick, any crafted instrument:
that some human touch might tap

the slow vibrato of a voice
that hadn't, all those years,
found a voice

and sat there waiting for release
as if it were the seed, the embryo
of all you knew, all that was carved

or strung unsung in you—
hardwood, horsehair,
cat-gut strings,

the pang of hunger
in the belly of a mammal,
sway of the living tree.

The Aftertouch

The skill of touching lies in the extremities:
lips, tits, fingertips, long-loosened hair,
though often there seems nothing much to share.

The dull, the sharpest eye, wanders where
along the edge a central feeling flares.
The skill of touching lies in the extremities.

I know from my own loves, from history,
the passion of the powers spilled in colonies
where often there seemed nothing much to share.

I know from those who touched too long, too deeply,
who scarred the inner properties of their care,
the skilled lies of touching in extremities.

Down the heart's harsh subway, this cold year,
the dumb cries of the blanketed poor rise.
I find there, finally, nothing much to share.

Love's the sealed border between two bodies,
of air, flesh, and water, of earth and fire.
Its skilled touch lies in our extremities,
then seams like nothing there, radiant and shared.

Zoo

All right, then, your husband must have found you dead.
What is that to me? It's only
the spirit gone out of the lonely body.
It's the uncontrollable kite
of anonymity floating above your life
like a buzzard out of some myopic sky
come down to swallow you. Now,
I'd say it's six short months
before the hospital, the two of us
laughing ourselves silly till the coke ran out,
your husband finding the pieces of yourself
in the stunned smile of another mouth.

Then the doctors hovered over you, stared down
at your thin, shaved mound:
The tents of caterpillar nesting in your womb
had been cut out or burned
or turned to gypsy moths and flown.
One enormous eye exposed
you, your legs somewhere above the room,
strapped in stirrups, floating through
the grin of drugs the aestheticians
of your life had given you.
They looked up you. And when they let you go
I dragged you off because your husband knew

not much could happen at the Houston zoo.
We went to see the sea anemone.
As always, they flowered bloomlessly.
Outside the aquarium, the baboons'
rainbowed genitals advertised themselves.
We threw them limes and oranges.
We made a mess. You were once
half-deaf. The day I heard I drove

back down: the goldfish
churned the pond. For every crumb I threw
one hundred pulsing mouths
rippled the one reflection I had of myself.

for Joanie Lippolis (1958-1985)

Toward a Definition of Home
for Joanie, once again

I didn't know where you had gone.
Your apartment, as is common in Houston,
lay above the garage
as if in Texas we needed beneath us
four wheels like a keel to promise us past
the palm, the pine, the cattle ranch.
The garage lay open like a toothless mouth
and one flight up, where I walked around
the catwalk, peered in at the mute
translations of yourself, those empty
rooms, the vines and gourds carved along
your bed's headboard, your one
abandoned shoe, I knew how fully
I am an animal. All the monuments
to your sudden absence
cracked open their one scent. The blood
shrills. Now two years,
two thousand miles north of where
your fertile silence was riddled by some new tenant,

I walk around my childhood home. The cherry tree's
a stumpless hole, the rhubarb's gone.
And where my mother hoed while bees
hovered near the horns of spring,
where trees and flower beds
bared their breasts for them,
the garden's sunk to pavement and six
wooden tulips. I walk around
the new, old ground. The house rises up
like an empty ark.
Every joist and mortise, every room
divides itself in two:
There is only memory and the barely quivering

silence of always.
There's the brown room and the flowered one,
Siberia and Shangri-La—
They have their new names now.
And here, in the front yard, the one maple
that I gripped with the hands of a child

breathes as always in its quiet knowing:
I dug it up a sapling and buried it again,
I watered it until it took
my name. My mother measured
its three-pronged trunk
as if it were my thickening waist and arms.
Now I lay my head against the incar-
nations of such love.
I press my nose against your distant
window. And think of the way
we house such rooms, the way the mind
fears vacuums, how we people even
space and oceans, love the human quality
of God and dolphins, and one old woman
buries her dead husband in woolens
because his feet get cold.

IV. Last Scenes

Summer in a Large House

They heard at night whatever small complaints
the house had gathered, stored, some eighty years
of them, as if it had arthritis in
each limb, and creaked and cracked in wind, no wind,
the exponential growth of each slight sound
as long as they listened, hearts to the bedded dark.

Or rather *she* heard, and he heard what she heard
when she woke him to it: a chair that scraped
across the hardwood floors, and one night,
she swore, "Oh Suzanna," in hushed tones,
and sent him flashing up the attic stairs
to where, he knew, in years, judging by
the general disrepair, and webs and dust,
the light bulb dead, nothing human had been.
It started his heart working. But when he went
back to their bed, for the sake of sleep he chose
to wish away her fear, what might have been there:
"Nothing," he said, "absolutely nothing."
All night that night, cotton in her ears,
something substantiated by the dark
settled with the mist till the sun burned it off.

Then there was another place she'd never go.
Then, like a sudden itch in deer tick country,
though they found, each long evening, nothing,
the whole of that house crawled with possibility.
Then it seemed she heard her own voice only,
an echo, half an echo, what she once meant
to say, or thought, and had forgotten, and then
beneath its breath the house would utter it.
They burned dried sage, left dishes of tobacco
and mugwort around the doors and windowpanes,

and on their porch, though she had never quite
believed before, they hung, lined and starred,
in fourteen different languages the names for God.

And if it somehow steeled them, that tacked-on display,
as if they staked a claim for summer always,
was for each dusk, for each night's moon to say,
or the foghorns lowing lowing each cold morning,
or for the slowest hour of the evening
when far from the sleeping children, he'd slip himself
into a pure abandon. But how could she
make love to him whenever *they* were listening?
Too often the cry that he had hoped to hear
would come in the form of a distant slamming door,
or a voice so low it might as well have not
been there at all. Then always it was night again:
If he slept and didn't stir, still at a word

he held her when she asked, pressed into her
the rote illusion of some distant mass,
the only prayer he knew, of love and dust
and bread, and she recited after him
though neither one could say to what or whom.
And still it pulled, born of the one breath
that bent above them the cypress's silhouette
and drifting, drifting, unseen everywhere,
pitched forever, it seemed to them forever,
dark and near in the warped old eaves of the ear.

Cutting the Tree

...quicken me all into verb, pure verb.
—Seamus Heaney

Each year, one father and no mother,
the tractor pulling us through
on a flatbed to rows of evergreen
where we would kill our own.
Each year you would not eye
them up for touch or size, or listen
to your daughter, who'd choose
white pine, the sharp softness
of her mother. You gave
no quarter, and would not hang
angel or frosted saint
above some amputated trunk.

But the night of our first night the year
was snug in its twelfth month.
From my boom box we drank in
the anger in exile Prokofiev bit
into a violin. It might have been
your own sonata, in F minor,
the death in 1967
of your imprisoned father,
and all Beijing the self infliction
of a wound that year, and you
just thirteen, learning to tuck
some anger beneath your chin
and make it sing. You might have seen—

always the story changed—Red Guard,
or been one, beat or watched
or shrank in terror, or urged
the whippings on. Always the silent
voice of the father, always the children's

ear tuned to some ditty above
the taut dissonance of a parent's love.
And while they ask me how we will
keep it green, water it a while or so
then drag it down to the street
and let it go (a false flame
burning from each window),
they cannot share the only hymn
their father hears by heart this year:

Farewell to an idea, then, farewell…
Farewell to your vulva full of flowers,
the blessèd seed of my slow answer
answering still. And always,
in the cry I heard,
I never understood the word:
Farewell, farewell, that pure verb.

Mao's Sparrows

A woman I once thought lovely told me a story.
It has made me think, tonight, of my own bird:
Mao clapped his hands, and she clapped hers

for me, clapped and clapped again,
and this is what all China sang:
Millions of sparrows lifting up from the cities,

blurring up from the cracked fields.
There was a grain of treason in this.
Masses of people clapped and whistled,

banged wooden spoons against
their empty woks. The trick was to keep
them forever aloft. How long anyway

can such slight things keep wing?
The birds, from exhaustion, dropped.
In the politics of famine, in the ideology

of wheat and rice and scorn,
Mao was indiscriminate. The sparrows,
being what they were, carried off

in their slight mouths, seeds like songs
of labor they had lifted from the earth.
When they fell the crowds beat them

with brooms they had fashioned
from branches, as if they killed them
with their very homes. Then they ate

the first meat they had tasted for weeks.
Then the mathematics of pestilence
summed. It was the strangest way

to kill a bird, a small decision, a fiasco
on a scale almost unimaginable…
Tell us a story of when you were young,

my children ask me each evening
as I lay on the floor between them.
As they give themselves to the dark,

they must know that I am breathing
near them, as if there were trouble
outside our door, as if someone

were clapping now that she is three
years gone. So I tell them, tonight,
of my own wings, how once I went hunting

for anything that would twitch or moan
before the drunk hunger
of a seventeen year old. I think of it often:

There was nothing but air.
The first time I had ever shot a gun.
There were only the slightest birds and one

12 gauge shotgun. Afterwards
a single feather floated. So much buckshot
for such small prey. I do not know

what sort of bird it was. The sun at 9 P.M.
feathers through drawn blinds
and I am careful to leave out the part

of any real passion. For the sake of simplicity,
I ask them to think of it as a sparrow,
the twenty-ton truck of the Chinese Republic

spilling down a mountain,
and the Red Guard the only guardrail,
and each of them only a child, each of them

waving the handkerchiefs their mothers
had made, the initials of the dreams
their fathers had long betrayed

stitched into the corners. And when
the drunk driver bears down on them,
when he catches, in his rearview mirror,

what might be wings, and lifts his hands
from the slick wheel, and the truck goes over
from anarchy to a still order, and a red road

glistens on the silken black banner
of Modern Day China? Desire
kicks in the gun. And you, my children,

who have seen such things?

          A single feather floats.

A bird drops from the sky.

We clap to shoo away
all trouble from our lives…

Hawthorn

In England, the May tree...

Mine is the hawthorn, that from its living
and dead branches, sticks—syringe like—
its presence in. No sentimentalist
of my attempt to marry it
to suburban lawn and shrub, it is armed
against the fool wisdom
of approaching in shirt sleeves
the unpruned health of any plainly
post-Edenic tree. From the ladder top
I saw off what I can reach, beyond that
smack with a length of pipe
the highest of the dead branches.
Only when I am done, I notice
the bull's eye of a thorn,
blackhead buried a half-inch deep.
I tweeze it out less easily
than it went in. Then an hour's ache.
Who can say what I have just been
inoculated for or against?
Once, among all of its deciduous kin

I loved the drape from sky to ground,
the sway and symmetry of the one
willow of my childhood window.
Now I keep what has come
with a gnarled home, this crown of thorns
that Christ-in-the-body once wore.
And around it, the pink and white
in which that crown was cupped,
the syrupy scent men waved
in the medieval name of May
until it drugged their women,
opened their guarded blossoms.

On nights like this one, I would give
the right limb of sanity's own clipped tree
to hear them *Gone a-Maying,*
calling up the power of their greening,
Sweet May Tree, Mother of Jesus!
when *May Day! May Day!*
is what they might have better cried
flat on their backs under a barbed sky.

Chance has stuck me with them,
this wilderness that cannot take,
however propped and trimmed,
a single name. It's simply too much work
to rout them wholly from my yard,
bud that will not bear
fully my embrace,
balm of the peasant, rite of the priest.

Cat's Paw

Suddenly, that evening, before you ever knew
more than the ring of me, you had snow
and in your high rise building caught it
only as the cat probed
the arc of flakes as they flashed by
in the portion of the night a lamp lights.
The limit of the cat's desire, perched
on your indoor sill, was a brush
of glass, the wind gesturing in a dust
the housed cat would never touch.
From where you sat, in your
two-bedroom, lower tip of Manhattan,
the cat reached toward a movement
so delicate it morphed to water
in a moment's grasp. At least that much

spoke to us. What loneliness never wished
for a quick fix? Those nights I pressed
your number on my cell. My voice
bounced off some distant orbit, yours
zinged back, across three states
of ice and grass. My young children
one story above me, yours sleeping near
the curl of the cat, winter's snuff
lisping past, and the phone against
my skin, smooth as glass.
Before we finally clicked each other off,
the will-o'-wisp of old loves snaked in
the smoke and mirror of our banter.
We could almost see them as we talked:

Old men, old women sculpting the air
with their bare hands, scooping it in,
as if there were something living
they pulled down from the sky
or out from the clouds
of their own bodies,
as if in motion only they could
take it in as air, give it back
as breath. If not for you
it was for me 1998 again, the first
wedged light of a Beijing dawn.
But just try to bottle that! you laughed.

When I finally brought myself to ask,
you arrived here, for one day only,
in the blur of the New Year:
For moments only, it seemed a touch
had forgiven us, seemed no matter
that in the twilight of our kind,
at the far reaches of the human arm,
tip of the index finger,
the winter-dusted, turned-out-of-doors
dead once spun
the cracked gyroscope of the sun.
In the simmer of that damp day

each of us left out the view
your jarred window scarred in you,
the hooked stunt of the planes
and then the broken arrow, then
the long vacuous months (cat's paw)
at Ground Zero. In the drizzle
of my Ohio, the elm in the fireplace
burned like coal. Our innumerable
fingertips lulled us back to such
a place as this:

               embers, smoke,
and the slow cartography of ashes
as they lifted. Wine and beer
and bread. Then the year's first snow,
a spooned, crocked roast. We kept
our glasses full, had nowhere
in particular we wanted to go.
A good ten hours before the fat of it
dissolved in our mouths.

Blue Flame

February 2003

When the sun is rising and my seven year old
catches it through the trees, and we sit
at the table, his slow oatmeal, my slow jam
and coffee, a dull magenta aching
in the horizon's nook, and a sharp
steel-eyed blue above it,
and blue the hottest part of the flame,
I know we live under the light touch

of heaven's scam. Or is it our own
tempering, heaven's stain?
Something chars us down from there:
The day comes soft shoeing,
all doe-eyed, the womb's wonder
of the sky. But in its slow time,
what will the battered
yoke of the dawn
sizzle in each emptying house?

In a minute, from the microwave,
the green digital flash of a school day.

All is quiet here, but somewhere
the flick of a candle sears
through rafters. Somewhere,
half a day and half the world away,
the red flag of morning snaps
at half-mast above our own
holy fire as it conjugates itself
across a cross-less altar.
Not here. Not now. It is, after all,

Ohio, and given the state of things,
the thermometer quivers into single
digits and everything slips
to its opposite. Cold burns.
The morning's hot celestial wax
drips into the seal of our
rushed footprints. In the boy-warmth

of the kitchen, absent for a moment,
the wet of our breath against glass,
this stirred bowl, this daily crust.

The Word *Wonders*

In it there is *Won* and *Woe* and almost *wound,*
and *One* and *Snow.* There is *We* and *Red*
and *Wed* and *Son* and *Done* as in
it is over, finally, *it is finished,*
or *I am,* and the back door slams.
And through the ripped screen
where this one word appears, there slips
in a slap, not across
the face but on the back—*Well Done!*—
and a beer for the whole crew
that gutted the old home
and beveled the corners, taped,
mudded, painted the rock…
And it is *New,* which appears there also,
and there is *Drone:*
There is all that never yearned
for the wonders contained in a single word.

And there is *No!* and *Nor,* and *Den* and *Send,*
but there is also *dres,* which is as good
as *dress,* which is as good *Worn* or *Down,*
*Don*ned or a*dorn*ed or left in the *Dew*
and contains, therefore, a *Rose,*
all embellishment, all nakedness,
and *Rod* and *Rode* and it is good
that there is also *Sword* and *Doe*
and *Or* and *Sewn* and *So* and *Sew.*
The word that begins with the W
of the World tucks in even
the tiny *Wren,* the slightest thing
with wings, some sheet spread high above
the delight of a child you love
who hovers a moment in the entire

tent of her own laughter. Then evening
Nods, of course, to *Snore*. And there

is also *Node*, and *Sore*, in sickness
and in health, and sticking your *Nose*
right where it most belongs.
Let's not forget *Ode*,
or for that matter the *sonder*
that whispers beneath its breath
of the U that would make *sunder*,
which mutters, in its own turn,
of *thunder*, but only in vitro.
Or *Swore*, the stunned mug of anyone
whoever *Drew* openly the wounds
of this one word…. *Is* does not appear,
but should, or else defers
for the moment to *Ends* and *Wends*.
Forever there is *Nerd*
and of course the word *Word* appears
and always will, and *Sod*—

everything you ever lost when last
the *Rend* of this one bird
broke the bank and I was thinking
again of the sheer boredom
that pressed me as we sang
for the *n*th time
our somnambulant round
of *Life Is But a Gently Down
the Stream*… And the sheet that floated
on air settles finally
around some story of June,
and a *Dose* of evening,
and the *Drowned* house it contains:
A wonder of such soft light
that there is, in a word,
a yes and a *No*, and a *Row*,
and a house that slips like a listing ship

from dusk to dark. The only quiet there
is a cat that taps the insomniac
of all today, all tomorrow must endure.
Then *Doer* defers to *Dower*,
ticking overhead in the half-bent blades
of a fan of a summer you once meant
to fix. There in the wash of it,
the unflappable *Roe* have hatched
in the seaside print of the sheets
where for the last hour
your children have been fast asleep.
A curtain billows in the wind
of a word and all it contains.
And the blinds buzz on their *Own*
all night long, ever and again,
of *Ern* and *Owe, Eros, Sow, Endow,*
and since forever *New,* forever *Now.*

The Seventh Seal's Last Scene

And when the lamb had opened the seventh seal
There was silence in heaven about the space of half an hour…

Revelations 8:1

Now that the Apocalypse has gone
entirely out of fashion, still they gather,
the knight, the squire, and the others,
already underworldly around
their last supper. From where they sit,
reading the Book of Revelations,
it's six centuries before, and only
eleven years after Nagasaki. For me,
in 2003, it's a fifty-eight year reprieve
and the thrum of a new Holy War.
In a minute, Death raps one last time
on the castle door. When the squire
answers, no one but absence there.
Still, the moment is upon them.
Soon, almost everyone will begin
grace notes to a cacophony that rose
from the first curtain like a giant crow
cawing up from a dying animal.
Then the girl, who has said nothing
throughout the whirr of the entire film,
turns the flush of one cheek toward
a throb of light. As if she were in some
way central to the scene, the camera
repeatedly cuts to her. For a moment
no one sees. Then there He is,
the black-robed monk,
the moon of his chalked face waxing.

Before the daunt of such a guest
wisdom's quick to keep its own counsel.
The girl leans toward the one line
Bergman allows her. The knight lifts

92

logarithms of religion toward the ceiling
of a castle he long ago abandoned.
The squire glares back at him, offers
nothing but nothing's repeated rebuttal.
The blacksmith's wife draws near
to the comedy of her sins. Then,
when the knight's wife tries to shush
the babble, and bids Death welcome,
the girl spills out her four words, *It is
the end,* kneels and is silent beside them.
Until that last moment, her horror,
her thanks, what joy she can feel,
are sealed. Sealed when the priest
tries to rape her, and she is quiet also

before the farce of the holy family,
Jof, Mia, those wandering minstrels
and their baby, who offer up
the swirl of the moment's succulence
in their gift of a bowl of berries.
The knight tongues it red in the thick
light of dusk. And when the flagellants
of desire sing their only hymn
and the soul's staked burning to a tree,
when the moth of plague
draws to the pyre
of a candle that licks lust's silk altar,
an awe that it should be like this,
a centered inward watchfulness
rides behind the cynicism of the squire.
From the back of his horse,
the girl wraps her arms fast.
What word could she utter, what act
might match the lost gambit
of the squire's laugh?
Only the minstrels escape, slip off under

the wagon cover of the knight's sacrifice.
In the span of that dark hour,
Mia shelters her only child in the scrim
of her family's calling. Then the coda
of her husband's vision,
so whimsical it is almost funny,
the monk and everyone
line-dancing along the horizon.
Still, it is strange how silence wins
always its own way in the end.
The Angel of Death—i.e., 1956—
dominates the final scene,
lifts one black, melodramatic wing
above the charred slump
of human flesh. Mum's the word
from the very beginning, the girl's
one song: Dust in its mouth,
more in the manner of the mole's
low hymn than of anything winged,
it drills its lulled way down to the blind
caverns of the skull, prods its dark
maw along the wild-eyed ditch-edge
of love and all new wounds—
Baghdad, Battery Park City, Kabul.

Slow It Down, Baby!

The cosmic expansion should have been slowing down a lot or a
little—an effect that should have shown up as distant super-
novas looking brighter than you would expect compared with
closer ones. But, in fact, they were dimmer—as if expansion
were speeding up. The universe was indeed speeding up.
—Time Magazine

They stared hard. The software didn't blink.
Light spun from the original yarn.
Those distant supernovas pulsed
more closely to the surge
of the first flash. So why, then,
did they thermo more dimly
than nearer Earth's own peripheral yard?

Out on the edge, things were heating up.
The warp of the Big inner urban Blast
didn't fizz in the lonely burbs of time.
Some dark energy—something we couldn't see—
kept churning, churning, as if the *Wonders
of the Unseen World* dusted itself off
and Cotton Mather beamed himself a spot

aboard the starship *Enterprise.*
The farther from matter's compact start
the faster the cosmos throws open the throttle
of a brand-spanking, good-as-new
trillion-year-old Ferrari.
But who needs the laser show of the heavens
for such a world-breaking story?

In the beginning, or near, we each sat through
the infinite first days of June, and yawned
for the blessèd break. When it came,
the weight of September massed behind

distant pine. Lithe bodies dove off
a pressure-treated dock. Out on the edge,
our old Sun minded its own spangled business.

Then the years bullied each slack season,
until a generation ganged up like this:
half-life half-spent in the light
chaos of kids. A kitten barely whines
before it wizens and dies.
A house floats by,
a dog staked barking to a distant ash.

Then all the left lane down to Columbus,
my daughter's mouthing, *Slow It Down,
Baby!,* the *Spice Girls'* drilled prophecy.
June is one fresh breath of air away.
It's in the stars, how time
will peter, how the loins' turbo charge
won't stick, the eternal engine burning

like nothing its last ounce of gas.
Old enough by then to be a child
in a line of children again,
I will find my place at the end
of the cracked whip. My feet will lift.
Faster and faster, at their late hour,
the furthest stars spin, sparks

of the party, drunks on a binge.
We have them in our sights now,
the brilliance of their abandon,
a fever more flush than ever
at the downy start. Then off the charts.
Then the hushed centrifugal wonder
of the drift of the dark.

Stephen Haven is Professor of English and Director of the MFA in Creative Writing Program at Ashland University, where he also directs the Ashland Poetry Press. He was educated at Amherst College, the University of Iowa, and New York University. His poetry and essays have appeared in *Crazyhorse, American Poetry Review, Salmagundi, Image, Western Humanities Review, Literary Imagination,* and in many other journals. Haven lives in Ashland, Ohio, with his wife Terri and their many children.